JOHN BYRNE WAS BORN IN DUBLIN, IRELAND IN 1963. HE HAS BEEN DRAWING CARTOONS FOR NEWSPAPERS, BOOKS AND ON TV EVER SINCE. HE ENJOYS 1 THING MORE THAN DRAWING and that's Teaching OTHER PEOPLE TO DRAW... people JUST LIKE YOU!

Draw your own face in here!

Some other books by John Byrne

The World's Scariest Joke Book
The World's Deadliest Joke Book
The Ultimate Joke Handbook
Crazy Classroom Joke Book

In the summer of 2002, Nickelodeon ran a
cartoon drawing competition in conjunction
with Puffin Books, and judged by John Byrne.
Puffin Books would like to thank all the staff
at Nickelodeon, particularly Neil Bennett and
Joe Godwin, for their help and support.

CREATE YOUR OWN CARTOONS

JOHN BYRNE

PUFFIN BOOKS

For Amanda Baptiste
5 Corinthians v17

PUFFIN BOOKS

Published by the Penguin Group
Penguin Books Ltd, 80 Strand, London WC2R 0RL, England
Penguin Putnam Inc., 375 Hudson Street, New York, New York 10014, USA
Penguin Books Australia Ltd, 250 Camberwell Road, Camberwell,
Victoria 3124, Australia
Penguin Books Canada Ltd, 10 Alcorn Avenue, Toronto, Ontario, Canada M4V 3B2
Penguin Books India (P) Ltd, 11 Community Centre, Panchsheel Park,
New Delhi – 110 017, India
Penguin Books (NZ) Ltd, Cnr Rosedale and Airborne Roads, Albany,
Auckland, New Zealand
Penguin Books (South Africa) (Pty) Ltd, 24 Sturdee Avenue,
Rosebank 2196, South Africa

Penguin Books Ltd, Registered Offices: 80 Strand, London WC2R 0RL, England

www.penguin.com

First published 2003
3

Made and printed in England by Clays Ltd, St Ives plc

British Library Cataloguing in Publication Data
A CIP catalogue record for this book is available from the British Library

ISBN 0–141–31507–5

INTRODUCTION

WELCOME! YOU'RE JUST IN TIME... I'M PUTTING THE FINISHING TOUCHES TO A CARTOON BOOK LIKE YOU'VE NEVER SEEN BEFORE!

YOU SEE, WHEN I STARTED LEARNING TO CARTOON, I READ LOTS OF 'HOW TO' BOOKS, BUT THEY WERE FULL OF FINISHED DRAWINGS AND I DIDN'T KNOW WHERE TO START...

...SO IN THIS 'HOW TO' BOOK YOU'LL FIND ALL MY DRAWINGS - THE GOOD ONES, THE 'MISTAKES' THE SECRET STUFF ONLY REAL CARTOONISTS KNOW! NO MATTER WHAT STAGE YOU'RE AT IN DRAWING YOU'LL FIND SOMETHING HERE TO HELP. SO GRAB A PEN AND SOME PAPER AND LET'S GET BUSY!!

TOP TIPS

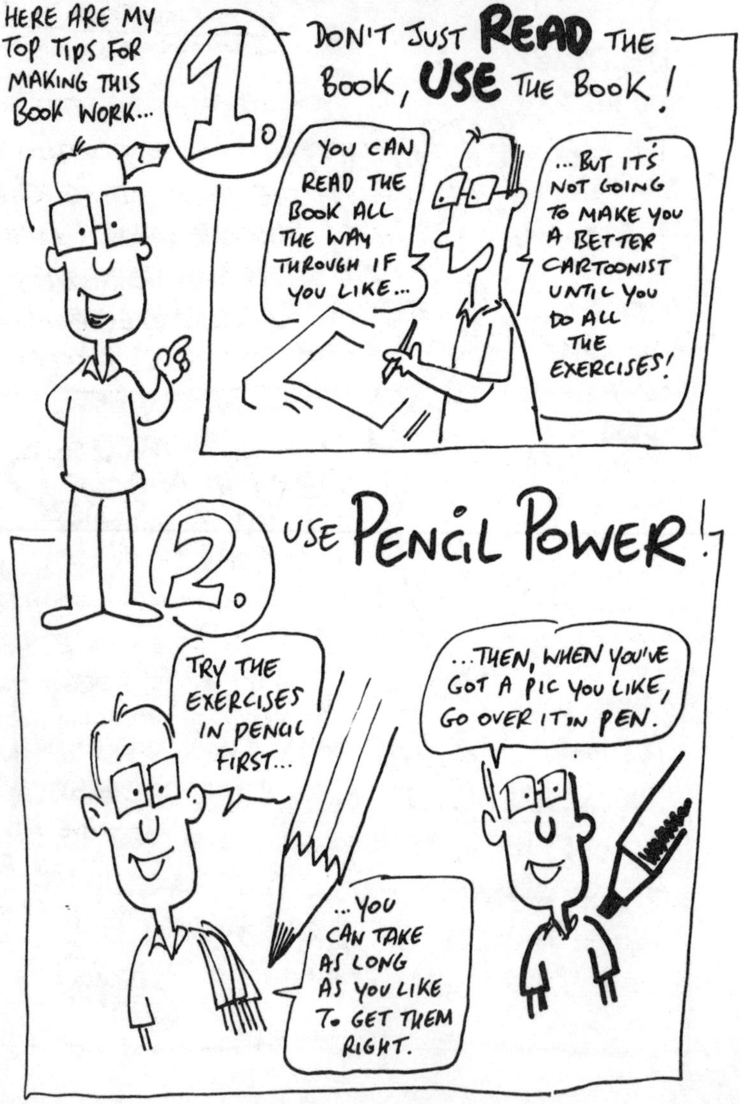
HERE ARE MY TOP TIPS FOR MAKING THIS BOOK WORK...
1.
DON'T JUST **READ** THE BOOK, **USE** THE BOOK!
YOU CAN READ THE BOOK ALL THE WAY THROUGH IF YOU LIKE...
...BUT IT'S NOT GOING TO MAKE YOU A BETTER CARTOONIST UNTIL YOU DO ALL THE EXERCISES!
2.
USE PENCIL POWER!
TRY THE EXERCISES IN PENCIL FIRST...
...YOU CAN TAKE AS LONG AS YOU LIKE TO GET THEM RIGHT.
...THEN, WHEN YOU'VE GOT A PIC YOU LIKE, GO OVER IT IN PEN.

3. DON'T WORRY ABOUT MIST~~AI~~KES

MIST~~AY~~KES ~~MUCKING THINGS UP~~

AS YOU WORK THROUGH THIS BOOK YOU WON'T GET EVERYTHING RIGHT THE FIRST TIME. GUESS WHAT: NEITHER DO I! MAKING MISTAKES IS THE BEST WAY TO LEARN... SO THE MORE YOU MAKE THE CLOSER YOU ARE TO SUCCESS!!

4. HAVE FUN!!

WHOOPEE!

YOU CAN'T EXPECT ANYONE ELSE TO ENJOY YOUR TOONS IF YOU DON'T ENJOY THEM YOURSELF.... SO MAKE IT PART OF YOUR JOB TO HAVE AS MUCH FUN AS POSSIBLE!

CARTOON SECRETS

This isn't a picture of Ugh Byrne, first ever cartoonist.
This is a T.Rex, last ever dinosaur to be cartooned.
Ugh Byrne is inside him.

Figure it OUT!

SECRET FILE
1
SECRET FILE

GUESS WHAT? YOU CAN ALREADY DRAW A BASIC FIGURE... IT'S THE GOOD OLD 'MATCH STICK PERSON' YOU'VE BEEN DRAWING SINCE YOU WERE VERY SMALL...

HANG ON! MATCHSTICK MEN ARE ALL VERY WELL...BUT SURELY THERE'S A BIT MORE TO CARTOON DRAWING THAN THAT?

YOU DON'T HAVE TO BE TOO MUCH OF A BRIGHT SPARK TO GET FROM A MATCHSTICK FIGURE TO A BASIC CARTOON FIGURE ... SIMPLY REPLACE THE 'MATCHSTICKS' WITH SAUSAGE AND BALL SHAPES!

HEY! THAT'S MORE LIKE IT!

PSST! IF YOU LIKE, YOU CAN START WITH A MATCHSTICK MAN IN VERY LIGHT PENCIL!

STAGE ONE:
DRAW THE 'BALL AND SAUSAGE' FIGURE. (USE PENCIL.)

STAGE TWO:
DRAW IN THE DETAILS OF FACE AND CLOTHES ON TOP OF THE BASIC FIGURE.

STAGE THREE:
RUB OUT THE GUIDELINES YOU DON'T WANT AND KEEP IN THE ONES YOU DO BY INKING OVER THEM.

ONCE YOU GET USED TO DRAWING OUR BASIC SHAPE, REMEMBER YOU CAN SQUASH IT OR STRETCH IT AS NEEDED...

FUN HOUSE

THIS TALL FIGURE MIGHT SUIT A BASKETBALL PLAYER... ... AND THIS ROUND ONE - JOHN AFTER TOO MANY PIZZAS.

BURP!

TOOL TIME:

Hi, I'M ONE OF THE MOST IMPORTANT DRAWING TOOLS - PAPER. TEAR YOURSELF AWAY FROM THE REST OF THE BOOK AND I'LL GIVE YOU SOME TIPS FOR USING ME!

1. DON'T SPEND ALL YOUR CASH ON EXPENSIVE DRAWING PADS - TYPING OR PHOTOCOPY PAPER IS A LOT CHEAPER AND YOU GET LOTS IN A PACKET

THE MORE PAPER YOU HAVE THE MORE PRACTICE YOU'LL DO...

... AND THE MORE PRACTICE THE BETTER YOU'LL GET!

500 SHEETS

PAPER

2. WHEN YOU'VE GOT SOME DRAWINGS YOU LIKE, KEEP THEM IN A STIFF-BACKED ENVELOPE... 'DOG EARS' ONLY LOOK GOOD ON DOGS!

cheek! -

3. DON'T FORGET THAT IF YOU FIND YOUR DRAWING IS TOO BIG FOR YOUR PAPER (OR IF YOU MAKE A MISTAKE IN ONE PART OF YOUR PIC), YOU CAN ALWAYS STICK TWO PIECES OF PAPER TOGETHER... THE JOIN WILL DISAPPEAR IF YOU PHOTOCOPY THE RESULT!

NO PROBLEM! HAVE YOU EVER BEEN WORKING ON A GREAT CARTOON AND THEN HAD JUST ONE BIT YOU COULDN'T GET QUITE RIGHT? OR MAYBE YOU JUST WANT TO MAKE YOUR BEST CARTOONS BETTER! WE'VE GOT LOTS OF CARTOON CLINICS IN THIS BOOK TO HELP YOU DO JUST THAT! WE'LL BE TAKING REAL PICS BY REAL PEOPLE AND OPERATING ON THEM BEFORE YOUR EYES... SO YOU CAN USE THE TIPS ON YOUR CARTOONS!

NURSE! SCALPEL, SCISSORS... SO I CAN CUT THIS STUPID MASK OFF AND SPEAK PROPERLY!

BYRNE

HERE'S A GOOD CARTOON FACE (WITH PARTICULARLY FINE TEETH!)

BUT HAVE YOU EVER FOUND THAT WHEN YOU TRY TO DRAW ONE OF YOUR CHARACTERS FROM A DIFFERENT ANGLE, YOU'VE BITTEN OFF MORE THAN YOU CAN CHEW?

By Antonia Atsiaris
Age 10

WHEN I DESIGN A CHARACTER I DRAW IN SOME PENCIL LINES LIKE THIS TO KEEP AN EYE ON THE SPACES BETWEEN DIFFERENT PARTS OF THE FACE OR BODY...

... THEN, WHEN I WANT TO DRAW THE CHARACTER IN A DIFFERENT POSITION IT'S EASY TO KEEP TRACK OF WHERE EVERYTHING SHOULD GO.

TRY IT FOR YOURSELF AND YOU'LL BE IN A POSITION TO DRAW EVEN BETTER CARTOONS!

GREAT CARTOONISTS TWO:
TOONTUNKHAMUN BYRNE
EGYPTIAN CARTOONIST

Toontunkhamun Byrne isn't wearing all
those bandages because he's a mummy.
Toontunkhamun Byrne is wearing all those
bandages because Pharoah didn't like his cartoons
any more than T.Rex.

Let's Face it!

SECRET FILE · SECRET FILE · **2**

NOW THAT YOU'VE DRAWN A BASIC CARTOON FIGURE, LET'S LOOK A LITTLE MORE CLOSELY AT CARTOON FACES..

YEUCCH! SOME CARTOONISTS HAVE FACES YOU WOULDN'T _WANT_ TO LOOK CLOSELY AT!

HERE ARE SOME VERY SIMPLE CARTOON FACES. IF YOU CAN DRAW SOMETHING SIMILAR (YOU CAN PICK THE EYES AND NOSES YOU LIKE), YOU'RE WELL ON YOUR WAY TO BRINGING CARTOONS TO LIFE!

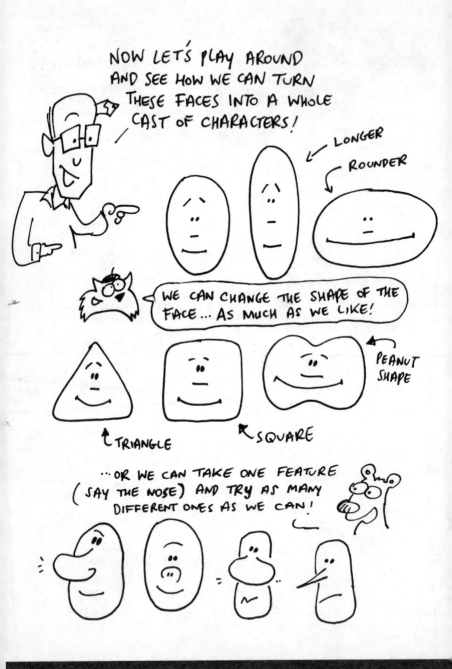

NOW LET'S PLAY AROUND
AND SEE HOW WE CAN TURN
THESE FACES INTO A WHOLE
CAST OF CHARACTERS!

← LONGER

ROUNDER

WE CAN CHANGE THE SHAPE OF THE
FACE ... AS MUCH AS WE LIKE!

PEANUT
SHAPE

TRIANGLE   SQUARE

... OR WE CAN TAKE ONE FEATURE
(SAY THE NOSE) AND TRY AS MANY
DIFFERENT ONES AS WE CAN!

TIRED
HAPPY
HERE ARE A FEW MORE FUNKY FACES. HOW MANY CAN YOU COME UP WITH?
DAZED
NOTE THE 'ONE EYE UP, ONE EYE DOWN' EFFECT... (ALWAYS GETS A LAUGH!)

OUCH! DARK CLOUDS AND THUNDER SHOW I'VE GOT A HEADACHE!
SOB! TEARDROPS FLYING ABOUT TELL YOU I'M S-SAD... AND SO I SHOULD BE – THE ONIONS FOR THIS DEMONSTRATION COST A FORTUNE!
HEARTS IN THE EYES AND EVEN A HEART POUNDING OUT OF MY CHEST SHOW I'M IN LURVE!
WHO WITH?
EVERYONE WHO BOUGHT THIS BOOK FOR A START!
MONEY SIGNS IN MY EYES SHOW I'M THINKING OF HOW RICH I'LL BE WHEN YOU LOT BECOME CARTOONISTS AND SEND ME GRATEFUL FIVERS THROUGH THE POST!
NOW SEE IF YOU CAN INVENT SOME EMOTION SYMBOLS OF YOUR OWN!

TOP CART

DO MAKE LOTS OF FACES YOURSELF TO SEE EXACTLY WHAT TO DRAW

DO NOT MAKE THESE FACES ON THE BUS OR YOU'LL SCARE THE OTHER PASSENGERS.

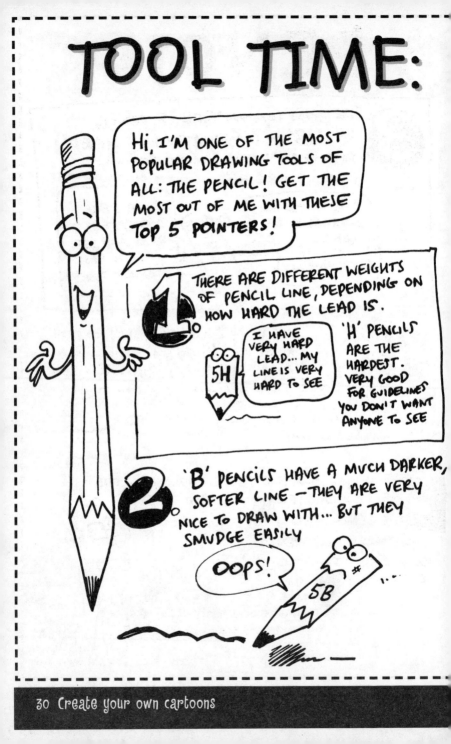

TOOL TIME:

Hi, I'M ONE OF THE MOST POPULAR DRAWING TOOLS OF ALL: THE PENCIL! GET THE MOST OUT OF ME WITH THESE TOP 5 POINTERS!

1. THERE ARE DIFFERENT WEIGHTS OF PENCIL LINE, DEPENDING ON HOW HARD THE LEAD IS.

I HAVE VERY HARD LEAD... MY LINE IS VERY HARD TO SEE

5H

'H' PENCILS ARE THE HARDEST. VERY GOOD FOR GUIDELINES YOU DON'T WANT ANYONE TO SEE

2. 'B' PENCILS HAVE A MUCH DARKER, SOFTER LINE — THEY ARE VERY NICE TO DRAW WITH... BUT THEY SMUDGE EASILY

OOPS!

5B

PENCIL

3 THE MOST COMMON TYPE OF PENCIL IS 'HB' A COMBINATION OF HARD AND SOFT LEAD... MOST SCHOOL PENCILS ARE HB.

> CHECK AND SEE WHAT KIND OF PENCIL YOU'VE GOT...

> TRY A FEW DIFFERENT ONES AND SEE WHICH IS BEST FOR YOUR TOONS!

4 ORDINARY SCHOOL ERASERS OFTEN RUIN YOUR DRAWING PAPER... TRY A SOFTER PUTTY RUBBER. (YOU CAN BUY ONE FROM AN ART SHOP.)

plastic

PUTTY

5 IF YOU HOLD YOUR PENCIL LOOSELY BY THE END AND FLOP YOUR HAND UP AND DOWN, YOU CAN MAKE YOUR PENCIL LOOK LIKE IT'S MADE OF RUBBER!

> THIS WON'T IMPROVE YOUR DRAWINGS MUCH, BUT IT LOOKS PRETTY COOL!

THE CITY IS A PRETTY COMMON BACKGROUND FOR CARTOON CHARACTERS... BUT WITH A FEW LINES YOU CAN MOVE YOUR CHARACTER TO EVEN MORE EXCITING PLACES.

By Felix Winder
Age 6

A HOT DESERT DOESN'T NEED MANY LINES AT ALL... DON'T FORGET TO ADD SHADOWS...

HERE'S A SPOOKY GRAVEYARD BACKGROUND!

RIP

YOU COULD ALSO ADD A CASTLE IN SILHOUETTE LIKE THIS. SHADING IT IN MAKES IT LOOK SCARIER...AND SAVES YOU DRAWING DETAILS!

SEE HOW JUST A FEW BRICKS GIVE A WALL EFFECT WITHOUT HAVING TO DRAW THEM ALL?

NOTICE HOW THESE PEN STROKES GIVE A GLASS EFFECT!

BYRNE THE BUILDER, CAN HE FIX IT?

YES HE CAN - FIX IT FOR HIM TO DO LESS WORK!

GREAT CARTOONISTS THREE:
THOR BYRNE

Oops! This isn't Thor Byrne, we're afraid. You know when they say 'The pen is mightier than the sword'?? This is the guy who proved to Thor Byrne that this saying isn't true when you're in a sword fight.

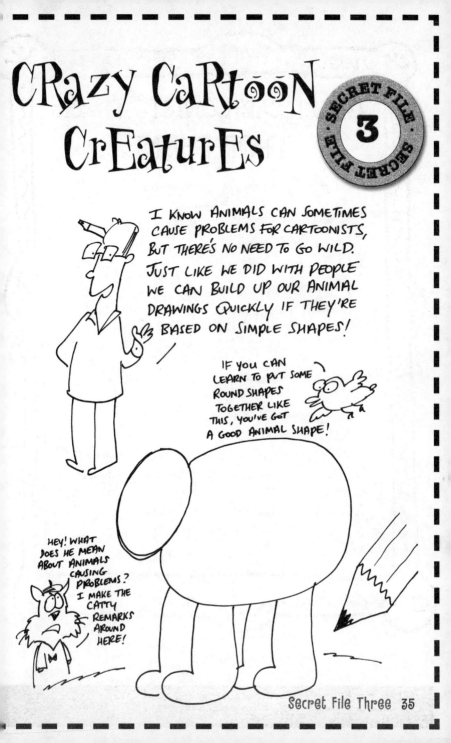

CRazy CaRtooN CrEaturEs

SECRET FILE · SECRET FILE · **3**

I KNOW ANIMALS CAN SOMETIMES CAUSE PROBLEMS FOR CARTOONISTS, BUT THERE'S NO NEED TO GO WILD. JUST LIKE WE DID WITH PEOPLE WE CAN BUILD UP OUR ANIMAL DRAWINGS QUICKLY IF THEY'RE BASED ON SIMPLE SHAPES!

IF YOU CAN LEARN TO PUT SOME ROUND SHAPES TOGETHER LIKE THIS, YOU'VE GOT A GOOD ANIMAL SHAPE!

HEY! WHAT DOES HE MEAN ABOUT ANIMALS CAUSING PROBLEMS? I MAKE THE CATTY REMARKS AROUND HERE!

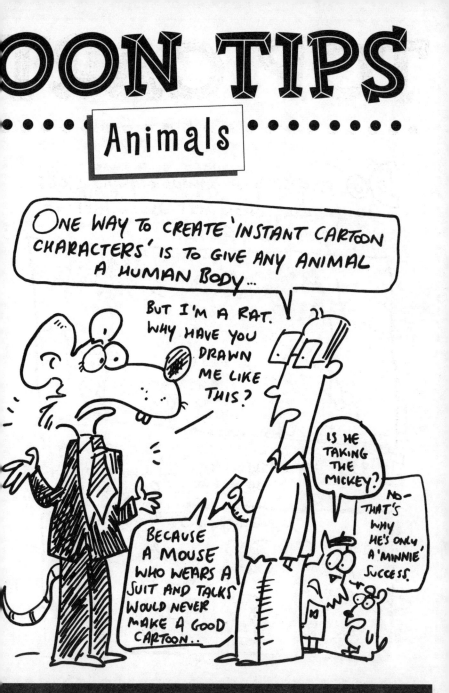

TOOL TIME:

NO MATTER WHAT SORT OF PEN YOU USE, HERE ARE SOME TOP TIPS TO HELP YOU GET IT 'WRITE'.

1 IF YOU'RE USING FELT-TIP PENS MAKE SURE YOU KEEP THE TOPS ON WHEN YOU'RE NOT USING THEM... EVEN FOR A SHORT TIME.

I'M COFF DRYING UP!

2. CHECK YOUR PEN ISN'T THE KIND THAT GOES THROUGH THE PAPER (AND IF IT IS, MAKE SURE YOU DON'T LEAVE YOUR BEST DRAWINGS UNDERNEATH!)

ARRGH!

OOPS... SORRY.

PENS

OH NO...
SO 'SMEAR'
AND YET SO
FAR!

MAKE SURE YOUR INK IS DRY
BEFORE RUBBING OUT PENCIL
LINES UNDERNEATH.

REMEMBER
THAT YOU CAN
AVOID YOUR DRAWING
LOOKING TOO DARK
BY USING CRISS-CROSS
LINES (CALLED
'CROSS HATCHING')
LIKE THE ONES ON MY
TROUSERS... HOW
MANY CROSS-HATCH
PATTERNS CAN YOU
MAKE?

By Antonia Atsiaris
Age 10

...IN THIS PICTURE YOU CAN SEE THE ARTIST HAS PAID SPECIAL ATTENTION TO SMALL DETAILS LIKE THE SHAPE OF THE GLASSES. LITTLE TOUCHES LIKE THIS CAN MAKE ALL THE DIFFERENCE IN GETTING THE PICTURE TO LOOK LIKE THE PERSON YOU'RE DRAWING.

A POPULAR PHRASE THE SUBJECT OFTEN USES MAY ALSO GIVE A CLUE TO WHO THE DRAWING IS...

SHUT UP!

PSST! JESS, YOU MAY WANT TO CHANGE THAT PHRASE TO 'QUIET PLEASE' BEFORE WE PRINT THE BOOK!

By Jessica Townsend
Age 10

AND WHEN ALL ELSE FAILS, REMEMBER YOU'RE A CARTOONIST. YOU DON'T HAVE TO DRAW THE PERSON AS A PERSON. WHAT ANIMAL WOULD YOU TURN **YOU** INTO?

Mad Penguin

By Jade Taylor
Age 9

GREAT CARTOONISTS FOUR
SIR SKETCHALOT BYRNE
CARTOONIST OF THE ROUND TABLE

We know what you're thinking – this isn't Sir Sketchalot, right? Well, you're wrong. Unfortunately, Sir Sketchalot's helmet got wedged shut, so since he couldn't see to sketch anything during his entire time at Camelot, he probably shouldn't be in this gallery in the first place.

NOW I CAN BUILD UP MY USUAL CIRCLES AND SAUSAGES ON TOP OF THE MATCHSTICK FIGURE...
GREAT! MAKES A CHANGE FROM ME HAVING TO BUILD UP BY DOING PESKY EXERCISES.
WHEN YOU'VE GOT A DRAWING YOU LIKE, RUB OUT THE PENCIL MATCHSTICK MAN AND BE AMAZED AT YOUR ARTISTIC ABILITY!

HAVE A PRACTISE WITH MOVEMENT DRAWINGS OF YOUR OWN AND YOU'LL SOON SEE THAT USING 'MATCHSTICK MOVEMENT' YOU CAN DRAW ANY POSE YOU WANT...
SITTING
DANCING
FOOTBALL
SWINGING
SORRY, JOHN... IT HASN'T WORKED FOR ME...
ME, MR MATCHSTICK MAN... MY DRAWINGS STILL LOOK LIKE... ER... PIECES OF STICK.
EH?
UH-OH!
THIS CALLS FOR A CARTOON SECRET...
SHAME
NOT MOVING at all.

LUCKILY, YOU DON'T HAVE TO RELY ON DRAWING ABILITY ALONE TO GET YOUR PICTURES MOVING. THERE ARE SYMBOLS WHICH HELP!

LOOK HOW DRAWING THESE 'SPEED LINES' AND CLOUDS OF DUST BEHIND ME MAKE ME MOVE FASTER ..

PSST! LEANING THE BODY FORWARD HELPS TOO.

IF YOU FEEL LIKE JUMPING, A NICE 'BOINNNG' EFFECT LIKE THIS ONE DOES THE JOB!

... AND VIBRATION LINES LIKE THESE CAN REALLY SHAKE THINGS UP. HAPPY NOW?

HAPPY? I'M COMPLETELY MOVED!

OON TIPS

Movement

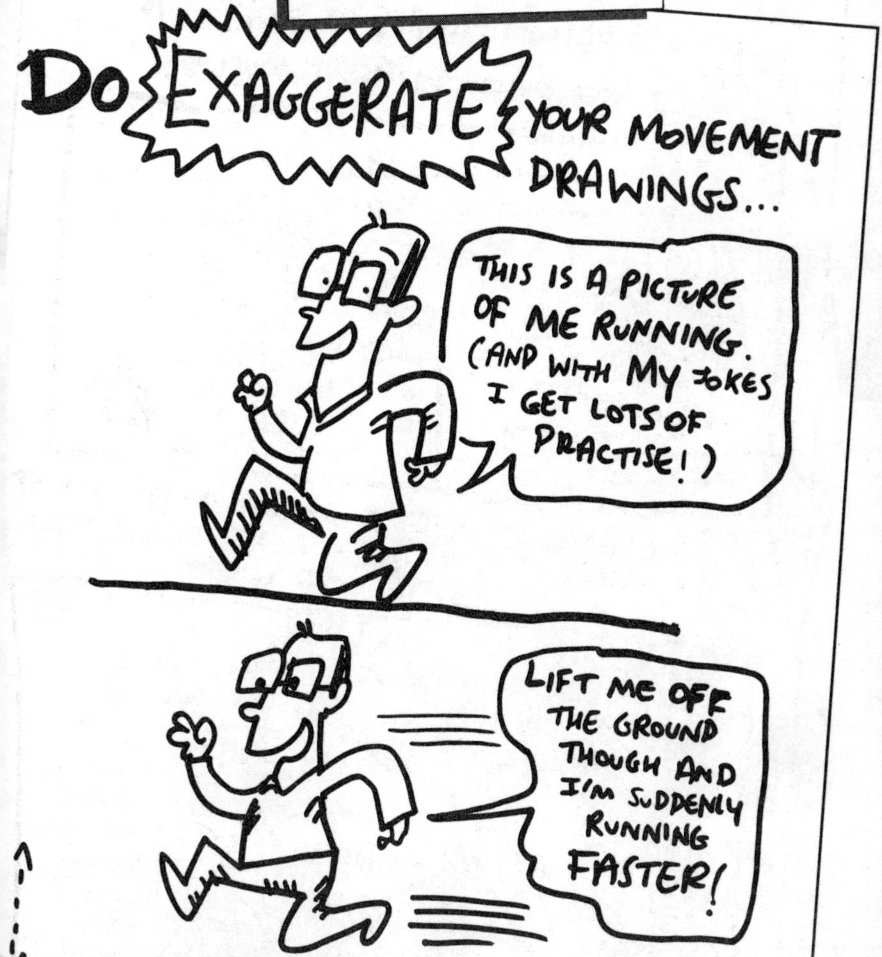

TOOL TIME:

I'M A BRUSH... MANY CARTOONISTS PREFER ME TO A PEN FOR INKING THEIR WORK... MAYBE YOU WILL TOO, AFTER YOU'VE BRUSHED UP ON THESE TIPS!

TIP NUMBER ONE IS, IF YOU'RE USED TO USING A PEN, DON'T TRY TO 'DRAW' WITH A BRUSH IN THE SAME WAY... EACH TOOL HAS ITS OWN STRENGTHS. EXPERIMENT TO FIND WHAT YOUR BRUSH DOES BEST.

THERE ARE SOME VERY EXPENSIVE BRUSHES AROUND... MAKE SURE YOU GET A CHEAPER ONE TILL YOU KNOW HOW TO TAKE CARE OF IT!

HAH! MY PRICE TAG SWEPT HIM OFF HIS FEET!

BRUSHES

3. BRUSHES ARE GREAT FOR FILLING IN LARGE BLACK AREAS, OR AREAS OF COLOUR, QUICKLY...

JUST MAKE SURE YOU LET EACH BIT DRY FIRST OR – YOU GET ME...

...THE DREADED SPLODGE!

OH NO!

4. MOST IMPORTANT OF ALL, CLEAN YOUR BRUSHES AFTER YOU USE THEM .... BUT

NEVER LEAVE THEM IN WATER!!

THIS APPLIES EVEN MORE IF YOU'VE BORROWED SOMEONE ELSE'S BRUSHES...

OTHERWISE YOU'LL BE FOR THE HIGH JUMP!

···CARTOON CLINIC FOUR···

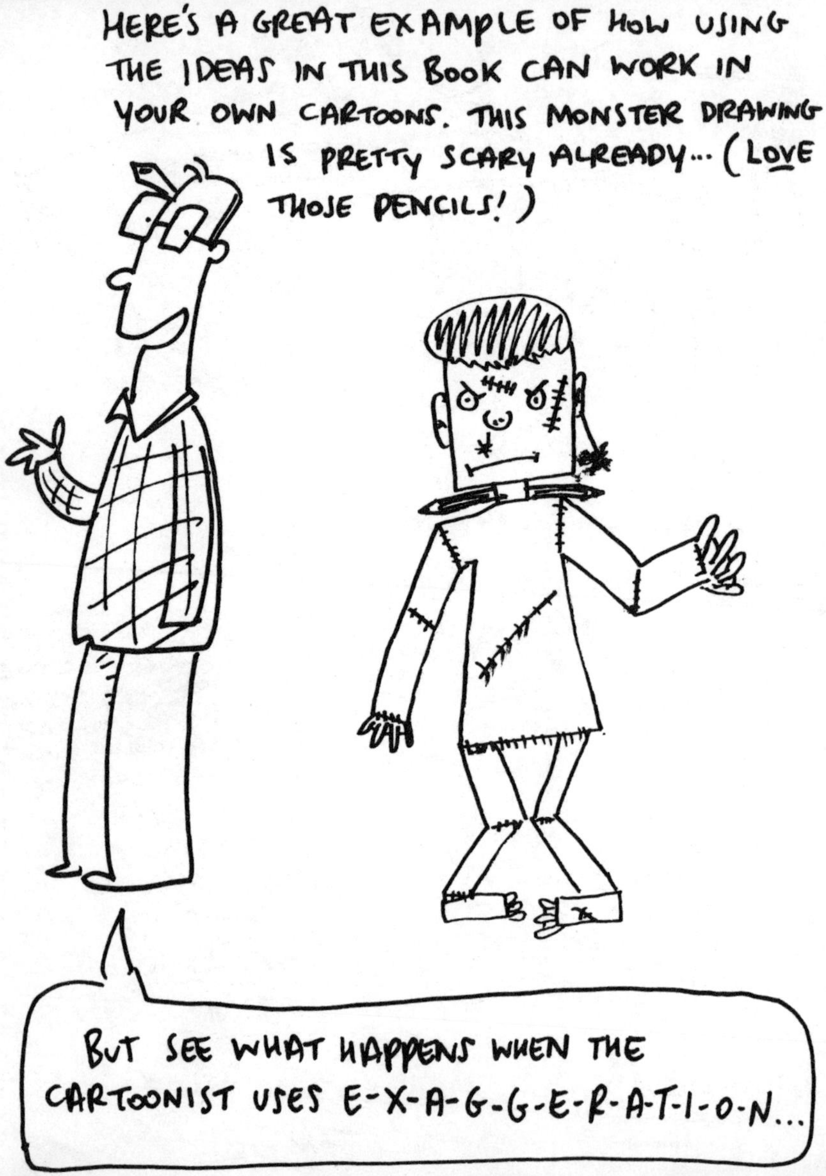

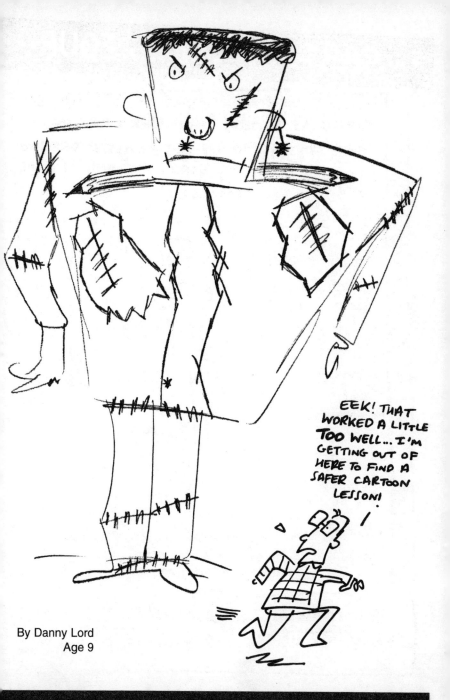

EEK! THAT WORKED A LITTLE TOO WELL... I'M GETTING OUT OF HERE TO FIND A SAFER CARTOON LESSON!

By Danny Lord
Age 9

GREAT CARTOONISTS FIVE:
MICHAELANGELO BYRNE

Michaelangelo Byrne was asked to paint cartoons on the ceiling of the Sistine Chapel in Rome. This picture is of another Michaelangelo who had to finish the job after Michaelangelo Byrne misheard the job as 'painting the chapel cistern' and locked himself in the loo for thirty years.

It's a Cartoon World!

ARRGH! DISASTER, DISASTER! STOP THE BOOK! WE'RE ALL DOOMED!

DO YOU MIND? I'M TRYING TO SPEAK TO MY CARTOON CREW HERE! THEY'RE GETTING REALLY **GOOD** NOW AND THEY'RE READY TO TAKE THEIR SKILLS TO THE NEXT LEVEL!

THAT'S THE PROBLEM! HAVE YOU SEEN HOW MUCH BOOK WE'VE GOT LEFT? WE'LL NEVER HAVE ENOUGH SPACE TO TEACH THEM EVERYTHING!

OH NO?

TRUE, THERE ARE SO MANY THINGS A CARTOONIST NEEDS TO BE ABLE TO DRAW, AND TO SHOW YOU EVEN HALF OF THEM WOULD FILL MORE BOOKS THAN I COULD EVER WRITE. BUT THE REAL SECRET IS THAT WITH THE **SAME SIMPLE SHAPES** WE'VE BEEN USING FOR OUR CHARACTERS, WE CAN CREATE A WHOLE WORLD FOR THEM TO LIVE IN.

BLUSH!

REALLY?

JUST FROM US?

TURN THE PAGE QUICK— THIS WE HAVE TO SEE!

BLUSH!

CIRCLES + BALLS

RECTANGLES + SQUARES

TRIANGLES + CONES

YES, ONCE YOU WORK OUT THE BASIC SHAPE, THERE'S NOTHING YOU CAN'T DRAW!
LOOK! THIS CYLINDER SHAPE CAN BE A TRAIN!
I CAN BEAT THAT... I CAN USE THE SHAPE TO DRAW A DRUM!
IT'S THE RIGHT SHAPE FOR A POST BOX!
POST

BOX CLEVER AND THIS BASIC SHAPE CAN BE REALLY HANDY...
EVERY CAR STARTS OFF AS A BOX...
THIS CAR WON'T START AT ALL...
BANK
THE BANK IS JUST A BOX WITH BITS ADDED... THAT IS HIS SECRET, YOU TWIT.
LET'S BREAK INTO THAT BANK AND STEAL JOHN'S CARTOON SECRETS...

PERSPECTIVE (OR MAKING YOUR CARTOONS LOOK LIKE THEY HAVE DEPTH) IS VERY SIMPLE IF YOU REMEMBER THESE RULES:

SOMETHING OR SOMEONE WHO IS <u>NEAR</u> TO YOU

WILL BE
1. BIGGER
AND
2. FURTHER DOWN THE PAGE

OON TIPS

Perspective

SOMETHING OR SOMEONE
WHO IS <u>FAR</u> FROM YOU

WILL BE

DRAWN

(1.) SMALLER

AND

(2.) HIGHER

UP ON THE

PAGE!

SO THE RHINO IS
SMALLER THAN JOHN
BECAUSE HE'S
FURTHER AWAY
FROM JOHN.

GOT IT?
HORNGRATULATIONS!

...SO I SUGGESTED HE TRY WORKING OUT THE BASIC POSE FIRST IN 'MATCHSTICK STYLE'...

...AND HIS SECOND DRAWING WAS A LOT MORE REALISTIC. ¿OUCH!؟ TOO REALISTIC IF YOU ASK ME!

WHACK!

GREAT CARTOONISTS SIX:
BYRNEY THE KID
FASTEST DRAWER IN THE WEST

Not him, of course. This is the guy they arrested after Byrney the Kid drew a moustache on all the wanted posters.

SECRET FILE 6 SECRET FILE

TURBO TOONS!

Crazy caricatures and amazing animation

ANOTHER GOOD WAY TO GET AN 'INSTANT CARICATURE EFFECT' IS TO DRAW THE PERSON'S HEAD NORMAL SIZE (YOU DON'T EVEN HAVE TO MAKE IT CARTOONY) AND THEN DRAW THE BODY A LOT SMALLER...

...AND ONCE YOU'VE LEARNED TO DRAW THE PERSON AS A PERSON, YOU CAN TURN THEM INTO THE ANIMAL THEY MOST LOOK LIKE.

WARNING: REMEMBER THAT ALTHOUGH IT'S FUN TO DRAW CARICATURES OF YOUR TEACHERS AND FRIENDS, HURTING SOMEONE'S FEELINGS ISN'T THE NAME OF THE GAME. BESIDES, A QUICK LOOK IN THE MIRROR WILL SHOW YOU THERE'S LOTS TO WORK ON IF SOMEONE WANTS TO GET THEIR OWN BACK BY CARICATURING YOU!

OON TIPS

Caricatures and Animation

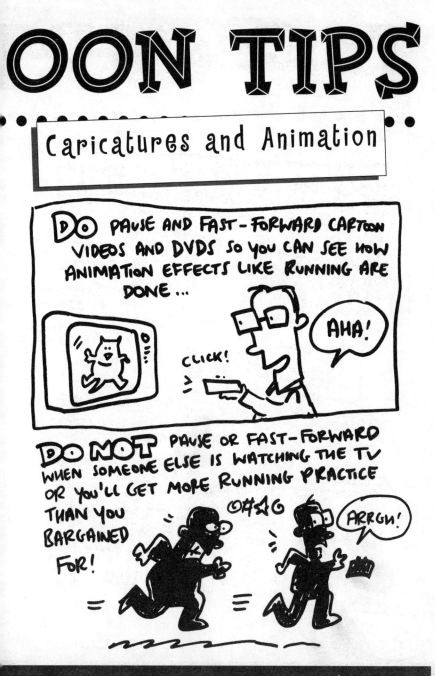

REMEMBER AS YOU WORK THROUGH THIS BOOK THAT THE IDEA IS TO GIVE YOU DRAWING TIPS... NOT TO GET YOU DRAWING EXACTLY LIKE ME.

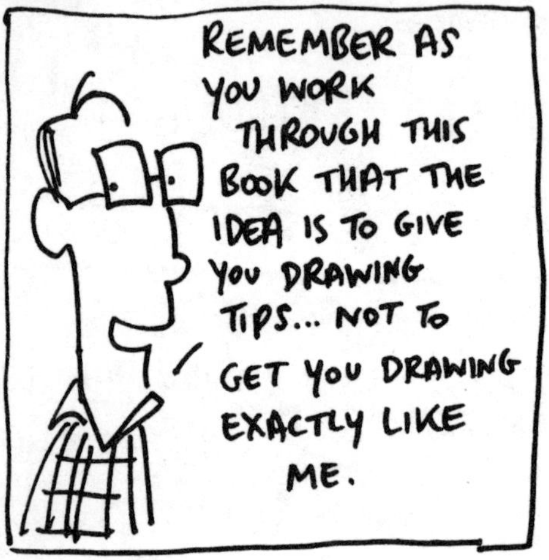

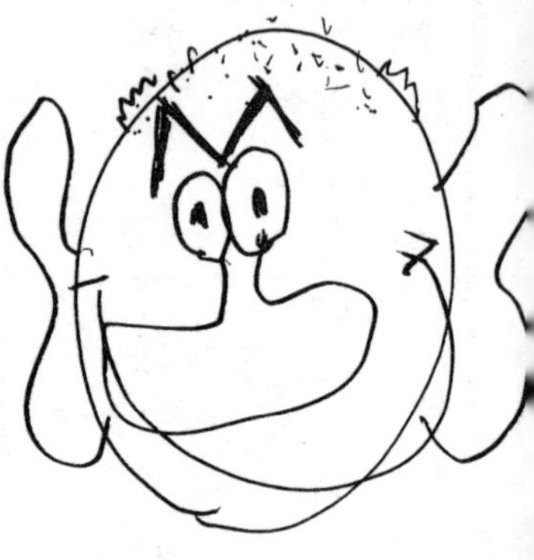

By Arnaud Fauchet-Baile
Age

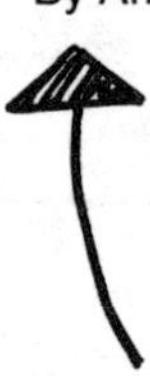

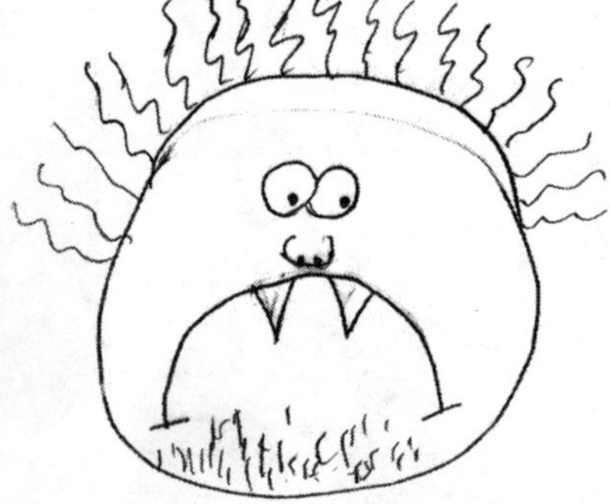

NOT THAT THERE'S ANYTHING WRONG WITH DRAWING LIKE ME, OF COURSE... MANY ARTISTS USE MY 'BALL AND SAUSAGE' WAY OF WORKING...

By Miranda Townsend
Age 10

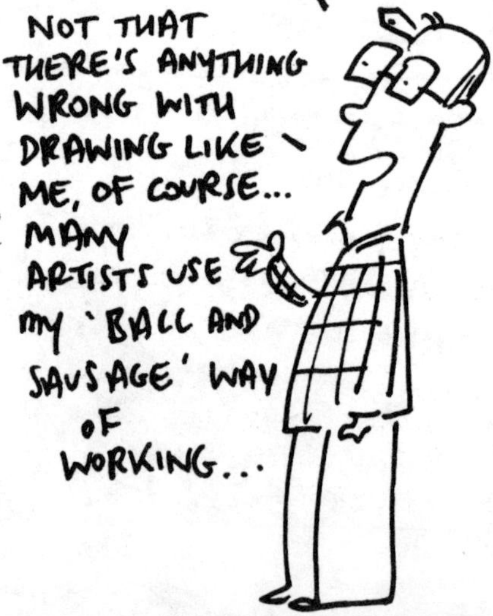

BUT TAKE A LOOK AT WHAT HAPPENS WHEN ARTISTS ADD THEIR OWN INDIVIDUAL STYLE OF DRAWING... MAYBE DIFFERENT TYPES OF EYES, OR A DIFFERENT SHAPE FACE.

By Solenne
Fauchet-Bailey
Age 7

By Jake Long
Age 8

...KEEP MAKING YOUR STYLE SPECIAL AND SOON PEOPLE MAY BE DRAWING LIKE YOU!

(DON'T WORRY, JOHN'S FACE WILL BE BACK TO NORMAL BY THE NEXT PAGE.)

(NORMAL FOR JOHN, THAT IS.)

GREAT CARTOONISTS SEVEN:
ROLF BYRNE
(THE FIRST BROADCAST CARTOONIST)

With the invention of broadcasting in the twentieth century, Rolf Byrne saw the chance to bring his own cartoons to a new audience. This isn't him but it is a clever Australian chap who waited for them to invent TV after Rolf Byrne proved cartoons don't work very well on radio.

John's Joke Box

NOW THAT YOU'VE MASTERED THE ART OF DRAWING COOL CARTOONS, YOU'LL NEED GREAT GAGS AND SUPER STORIES TO GO WITH THEM...

FOR OUR DRAWING WE USED CIRCLES, BOXES AND SAUSAGES. IN OUR JOKE FACTORY WE'LL BE USING IDEAS, THOUGHTS AND QUESTIONS. BUT DON'T WORRY. YOUR BRAIN ALREADY CONTAINS EVERYTHING YOU NEED. SEE? HERE IT IS NOW

CARTOONIST BRAIN

YOU'LL HAVE TO HELP ME OUT WITH THE NEXT FEW PAGES, GANG... AS YOU CAN SEE I'VE COMPLETELY LOST MY HEAD!

HERE'S A THREE PICTURE COMIC STRIP I DREW ABOUT SOMEONE WHO CAN'T GET TO SLEEP. I ASKED MYSELF 'WHAT COULD HAPPEN NEXT?' TO COME UP WITH THE LAST PICTURE...

... AND HERE'S THE SAME STRIP AGAIN, BUT THIS TIME I LEFT THE LAST PICTURE BLANK SO YOU CAN ASK YOURSELF 'WHAT COULD HAPPEN NEXT?' AND COME UP WITH AN EVEN FUNNIER ENDING!

WHEN YOU'RE DRAWING CARTOON ANIMALS TRY TO HAVE A LOOK AT THE REAL THING TOO — IT REALLY HELPS YOUR DRAWINGS. TAKE FINLAY'S FIRST DRAWING OF A BULL:

NOW, SEE HOW MUCH BETTER THE DRAWING LOOKS AFTER HE ADDED SOME REAL BULL BITS AND BOBS...

By Finlay Sinclair
Age 8

By Amy Czapnik
Age 10

NOW YOU'RE
THIS IS A 'SPEECH BALLOON' SO YOU CAN 'HEAR' WHAT I'M SAYING!
THIS IS A 'WHISPER BALLOON'... THE DOTTED LINE SHOWS I'M SPEAKING VERY QUIETLY.
IN THIS 'THINK BALLOON' I'M THINKING HOW IMPORTANT IT IS TO LETTER YOUR SPEECH BALLOONS CLEARLY... NO POINT HAVING GOOD JOKES IF NOBODY CAN READ THEM!

···CARTOON CLINIC EIGHT··

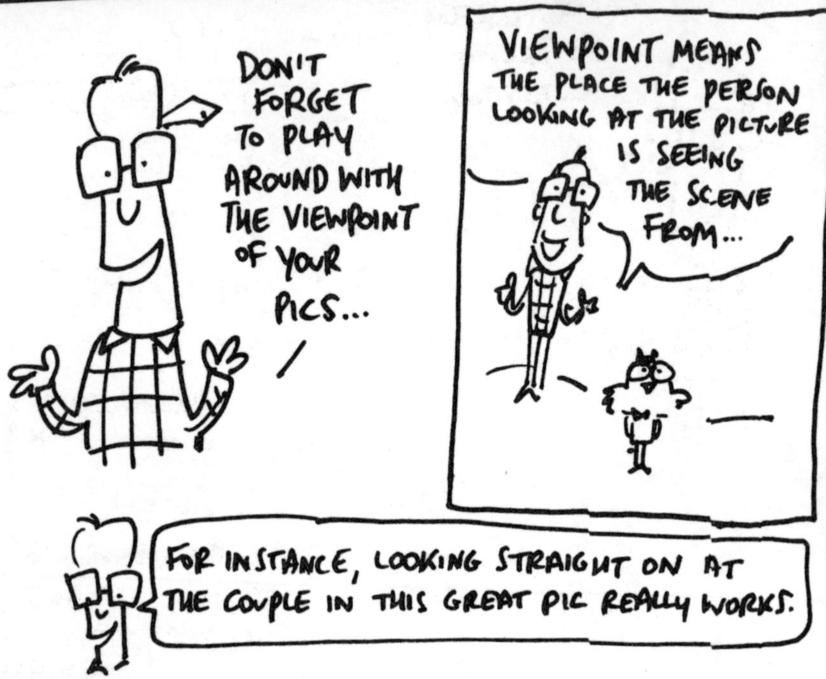

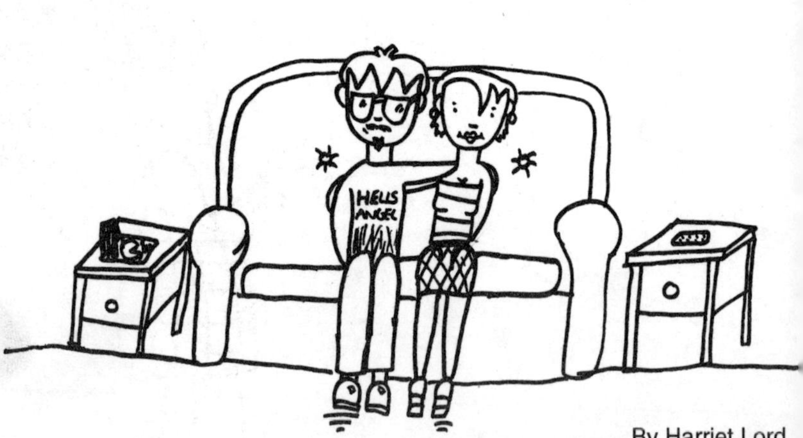

By Harriet Lord
Age 11

WHILE I THOUGHT THIS BUTTERFLY WAS PRETTY CUTE, TOO.

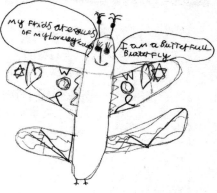

By Jerri-Leigh Trew
Age 7

... BUT CHANGING TO THIS 'UP AND UNDER' VIEW REALLY MAKES THE PICTURE TAKE OFF!

GREAT CARTOONISTS EIGHT:
FLASH BYRNE
23RD CENTURY CARTOONIST

This might look like T.Rex but it actually is Flash Byrne. Unfortunately he got mixed up with one of his own cartoons when he left it in the matter transporter.

OK, GANG... HERE'S A FILE FULL OF TIPS AND PROJECTS SO YOU CAN REALLY STRETCH YOUR TOONING SKILLS.

ON YOUR MARKS, GET SET...

GET TOONING!

BLAM!

ARRGH! WHY IS HE LETTING GUNS OFF IN A CARTOON BOOK?

HEY, MAKES A CHANGE FROM JUST SHOOTING HIS MOUTH OFF!

...AND SEE HOW SMALL YOU CAN REDUCE THE PIC TILL YOU CAN'T SEE IT AT ALL...

MOST COPIERS DO FROM 50% (HALF SIZE) TO 200% (TWICE THE SIZE)...BUT YOU CAN ALWAYS PHOTOCOPY YOUR COPIES ALL OVER AGAIN!

YOU CAN ALSO MAKE LITTLE PICS INTO **HUGE POSTERS!**

EEK!

← you may have to copy really big posters in BITS and stick them together

IF YOU REALLY LIKE A PICTURE YOU CAN COPY IT OVER AND OVER AND OVER AND OVER AND OVER AND OVER... OK, I THINK YOU'VE GOT THE IDEA...

NOW THAT YOU'RE GOING TO BE AN EXCITING NEW FACE ON THE CARTOON SCENE ...
... ISN'T IT TIME YOU CELEBRATED BY GIVING YOURSELF AN EXCITING NEW FACE?
WOW! COOL CARTOON MASK MAKING!

By NOW YOU MUST BE SICK OF SEEING SILLY CARTOON PICS OF ME ALL OVER THIS BOOK... SO WHY NOT TAKE A LEAF OUT OF ROWANS BOOK AND USE YOUR CARTOON SKILLS TO DO A SILLY CARTOON PIC OF YOURSELF?

By Rowan Fauchet-Bailey
Age 11

JB'S F.A.Q.S

IN CASE YOU'RE WONDERING, F.A.Q's ARE 'FREQUENTLY ASKED QUESTIONS' — THINGS I'M ALWAYS ASKED AT CARTOON CLASSES. I'LL ANSWER THEM AGAIN HERE ...

BET I KNOW WHAT THE 'J.B.' STANDS FOR, TOO

'JOLLY BALD'.?

I HOPE YOU'LL TAKE ALL THE TIPS AND TRICKS YOU LEARN IN THIS BOOK AND TRY THEM FOR YOURSELF... BUT DON'T JUST COPY MY WORK. THERE ARE LOTS OF EXCITING ARTISTS AND CARTOONISTS YOU CAN LEARN FROM. IF YOU'VE GOT A FAVOURITE ARTIST WHY NOT WRITE TO THEM (OR THEIR PUBLISHER) FOR ADVICE? YOU MIGHT FIND SOME OF THE ANSWERS ARE DIFFERENT TO MINE. THERE ARE NO WRONG OR RIGHT WAYS TO DRAW... ONLY WHAT WORKS BEST FOR YOU!

Q. ARE YOU DRAWING ALL THE TIME?

A. I USED TO...THEN I REALIZED YOU CAN HAVE TOO MUCH OF A GOOD THING, EVEN WHEN IT'S CARTOONS. I LIKE WALKING, SPENDING TIME WITH MY FAMILY AND I **LOVE** MUSIC (MY CD COLLECTION IS BIGGER THAN MY BOOKS AND COMICS PILE). I ALSO HELP RUN THE KIDS CLUB AT MY CHURCH. I FIND HAVING OTHER INTERESTS GIVES ME LOTS OF NEW IDEAS FOR MY CARTOONS WHEN IT'S DRAWING TIME AGAIN. PRACTICE MAKES PERFECT... BUT A CHANGE IS GOOD TOO. (unless you change into a werewolf, of course.)

Q. DO BOYS OR GIRLS MAKE BETTER CARTOONISTS?

A. GIRLS, BOYS, YOUNG, OLD ...
I HAVE TAUGHT, LEARNED FROM AND WORKED WITH CARTOONISTS OF ALL SHAPES AND SIZES. SOME, LIKE ME, STARTED OFF WHEN THEY WERE SMALL KIDS. OTHERS MIGHT BE A LOT BIGGER, AND STARTED FROM A BOOK LIKE THIS OR A SUMMER ART CLASS OR JUST A DESIRE TO 'HAVE A GO'. DON'T WORRY ABOUT WHETHER ANYONE IS 'BETTER' OR 'WORSE' AT CARTOONING. I PROMISE THERE'S NOBODY WHO CAN DRAW YOUR CARTOONS LIKE **You**!

WORLD'S BEST CARTOONIST

WE'VE KEPT A PLACE FOR YOU!

Q. WHO'S YOUR FAVOURITE CARTOONIST?

A. YOU ARE, COS YOU'RE READING MY BOOK! I LIKE LOTS OF CARTOONISTS... AND LOTS OF OTHER ARTISTS TOO. I THINK WE CAN LEARN SOMETHING FROM EVERYONE. (I'VE PICKED UP QUITE A FEW TRICKS FROM YOUNG ARTISTS WHO COME TO MY CLASSES!) I HOPE THAT AS WELL AS READING THIS BOOK YOU'LL CHECK OUT AS MANY OTHER CARTOONS AS YOU CAN... IF EVERYONE DREW LIKE ME IT WOULD BE A VERY BORING WORLD!

YAWN!

Q. WHAT'S YOUR FAVOURITE TYPE OF CARTOON TO DRAW?

A. OVER THE YEARS I'VE DRAWN MOST KINDS OF CARTOON...JOKE CARTOONS, COMIC STRIPS—BOTH FUNNY AND MORE SERIOUS—GREETINGS CARDS, PORTRAITS OF PEOPLE AND I ALSO DRAW LIVE ON TV. SOME THINGS I DO BETTER THAN OTHERS... BUT THAT'S ALL PART OF LEARNING. THE MORE CARTOONS YOU TRY, THE MORE CHANCE OF FINDING OUT WHAT YOU ARE GOOD AT.

(AND WHEN YOU DO MAYBE YOU CAN SHOW ME!)

MUM! JOHN'S DRAWING ON THE TV AGAIN!

WELL, TELL HIM TO GET OFF!

Q. WHEN DID YOU START CARTOONING?

A. I STARTED CARTOONING WHEN I WAS ABOUT FOUR... I USED TO DRAW CHARACTERS FROM MY FAVOURITE CARTOON MOVIES. I KNOW SOME ARTISTS SAY YOU SHOULD NEVER COPY...BUT I THINK IT'S A GOOD WAY TO LEARN. JUST MAKE SURE YOU USE THE TIPS YOU PICK UP WHILE COPYING TO DO YOUR OWN DRAWINGS. AND NEVER PASS OFF SOMEONE ELSE'S WORK AS YOUR OWN. TRUST ME, WITH A LITTLE PRACTICE (AND THIS BOOK) YOU'LL BE DOING DRAWINGS LIKE NOBODY ELSE CAN DO BEFORE YOU KNOW IT!

Q. WHAT'S THE BEST CARTOON YOU'VE EVER DONE?

A. I HAVEN'T DONE IT YET. JUST LIKE A MUSICIAN OR A SPORTS PERSON, A GOOD ARTIST SHOULD ALWAYS PUSH THEMSELVES TO GET BETTER AND BETTER. AND THERE ARE ONLY THREE WAYS TO DO THAT:

PRACTICE PRACTICE AND MORE PRACTICE

HOW TO BE GOOD AT SPORT

PUFF! PANT! ISN'T IT LUCKY THAT CARTOON PRACTICE IS FUN!

Q. COULD I GET A JOB AS A CARTOONIST?

A. WHEN I STARTED OFF CARTOONING IT WAS HARD TO GET PEOPLE TO SEE THAT 'DRAWING FUNNY PICTURES' WAS 'REAL WORK'. NOWADAYS YOU CAN SEE CARTOONS IN ADVERTISING, ON TV, IN VIDEO GAMES... YOU NAME IT.

GREAT! SO I SHOULD QUIT SCHOOL AND BECOME A CARTOONIST!

ER... **NO.** THE MORE YOU LEARN AT SCHOOL, FROM HISTORY TO SCIENCE, ENGLISH TO GEOGRAPHY, THE MORE IDEAS YOU'LL HAVE FOR YOUR TOONS. AND MATHS HELPS WITH MAKING YOUR CARTOON MONEY LAST UNTIL NEXT PAYDAY!

PS WHETHER YOU WANT TO WORK AS A CARTOONIST OR IT'S JUST A HOBBY, HAVING FUN IS THE No1 TIP!

Q. CAN I CONTACT YOU WITH MY OWN QUESTION?

A. YES, I KNOW JUST HOW YOU FEEL... I ALWAYS THINK OF MY BEST QUESTION JUST AFTER I'VE LEFT THE CLASS OR FINISHED THE BOOK. OR MAYBE I THINK THE QUESTION IS JUST TOO SILLY TO ASK OUT LOUD. YOU CAN CHECK OUT MY WEBSITE AT

WWW.WEBTOONIST.COM

use all small letters of course.

EVEN IF YOU DON'T HAVE QUESTIONS YOU'LL FIND FEATURES, CLASSES AND OTHER FUN STUFF! LOOK FORWARD TO HEARING FROM YOU!

LET'S FACE IT...

EVEN IF THIS BOOK WAS TWICE AS LONG, THERE WOULDN'T BE ROOM TO FIT IN ALL THE GREAT TRICKS YOU CAN PULL WITH JUST ONE PIC!

SAY YOU'VE GOT A FUNNY FACE LIKE HANNAH'S, BELOW *

By Hannah Long
Age 11

* ER...I MEANT HANNAH'S DONE A PICTURE OF A FUNNY FACE!

GRR!

↑ HANNAH

1. YOU CAN TRY CHANGING THE EXPRESSION... EYEBROWS AND MOUTHS ARE GOOD PLACES TO START.

2. ... YOU CAN ADD EYES OF A DIFFERENT DESIGN (AND NOSES, HAIR ETC) AND SEE HOW THAT LOOKS.

3. A FUNNY HAT CAN MAKE EVEN SCARY FACES SILLIER... I JEST NOT.

4. ... IF YOU'RE REALLY CONFIDENT, TRY DRAWING THE FACE FROM THE SIDE.

LOOK! HE'S GOT SIDE BYRNES!

SPEED UP

YOUR CARTOON SUCCESS!

HERE'S A FUN DRAWING OF A SKATEBOARDING SCRIBBLE THAT BARNABY DREW.. LET'S SEE IF WE CAN USE OUR CARTOON SKILLS TO GIVE HIM A SUPER SPEEDY TUNE UP!

By Barnaby Winder
Age 11

CARTOONISTS HAVE A WHOLE RANGE OF SYMBOLS TO SHOW SPEED, LIKE CLOUDS OF DUST OR SPEED LINES

LIFTING OBJECTS OR PEOPLE OFF THE GROUND AND ADDING SOME SHADOW UNDERNEATH ALSO HELPS!

GIVING BARNABY'S CHARACTER A LONG SCARF THAT TRAILS BEHIND HIM HELPS KEEP HIM MOVING....

ZOoooom!

YOU CAN USE THE LETTERS IN 'ZOOM' TO MAKE THE PIC SPEEDY... HAVE THEM GET SMALLER AS OUR HERO GETS FURTHER AWAY.. AND WE MIGHT AS WELL END THIS PAGE NOW, COS AS YOU CAN SEE, HE'S GONE!

HERE ARE SOME OF THE WINNERS
OF MY CARTOON COMPETITION ON
NICKELODEON TV. I'VE PUT THEM
IN THE BOOK JUST TO SHOW HOW
MANY DIFFERENT STYLES OF DRAWING
PEOPLE CAN HAVE. BUT JUST
BECAUSE **YOUR** STYLE
ISN'T LIKE ANY OF THESE
DOESN'T MEAN IT'S NOT
A **STAR** STYLE

TOO... READY? LIGHTS,
CAMERA, ACTION!

By Kirsty Williams
Age 14

By Judy Buckingham

By Rachel Banner
Age 13

By Amy Hill
Age 11

Ginger McGing

MUM: Big Red
DaD: Hamish
LiTTL sister: Ruby

Favourite
food: Hagges

Hobbies: Talking to
Lochness monster.
Best friend: Lochness
monster.
pet: Ginger tom cat

By Rachel McNeil

By Sarah Kotb
Age 13

Dave Berry.

Michelle.

NiCKEL

PRESENTERS.

By Robert Sumbland
Age 13

Yolly.

Rhani.

HERE ARE SOME
PICTURES BASED
ON REAL PEOPLE...
BUT STILL FUNNY
WHETHER YOU
KNOW THE
PEOPLE OR NOT!

SPOT

By Vicky Talbot
Age 12

By Michael O' Mahony

AWARDS TIME!

...AND THE WINNER OF THE AWARD FOR 'MOST CREATIVE CARTOONIST' IS... YOU!

HERE'S A REALLY IMPRESSIVE BADGE FOR YOU TO CUT OUT AND KEEP..

I Completed John Byrne's Cartoon Book

...AND HERE'S AN EVEN BIGGER ACHIEVEMENT!

I Survived a John Byrne Joke Book

This is to Certify that

....

Your name here

has successfully completed

and is now

licensed to cartoon at home, in school and in public.

Although ONLY on pieces of paper.
Graffiti drives us up the wall.

John Byrne

Thanks to EVERYONE WHO TOOK PART IN THE PUFFIN WORKSHOPS AND NICKELODEON COMPETITION TO PROVIDE PICS FOR THIS BOOK!

SORRY WE COULDN'T USE ALL THE GREAT DRAWINGS BUT YOU CAN SHOW ME YOUR PICS ON WWW.WEBTOONIST.COM MAYBE WE'LL EVEN USE SOME IN THE NEXT BOOK!

HAPPY DRAWING!

X

Even more mirth and madness with John Byrne

● ● ● ● ● ● ● ● ● ● ● ● ● ● ● ● ●

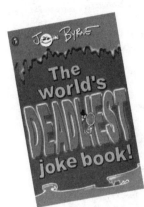

A collection of the most lethal jokes in the universe - and we're not afraid to use them.

Jokes that'll give you the screaming heebie-jeebies, and drawings to make you dive under the duvet.

Read more in Puffin

For complete information about books available from Puffin – and Penguin – and how to order them, contact us at the appropriate address below. Please note that for copyright reasons the selection of books varies from country to country.

www.puffin.co.uk

In the United Kingdom: Please write to Dept EP, Penguin Books Ltd,
Bath Road, Harmondsworth, West Drayton, Middlesex UB7 ODA

In the United States: Please write to Penguin Putnam Inc., P.O. Box 12289,
Dept B, Newark, New Jersey 07101–5289 or call 1–800–788–6262

In Canada: Please write to Penguin Books Canada Ltd,
10 Alcorn Avenue, Suite 300, Toronto, Ontario M4V 3B2

In Australia: Please write to Penguin Books Australia Ltd,
P.O. Box 257, Ringwood, Victoria 3134

In New Zealand: Please write to Penguin Books (NZ) Ltd,
Private Bag 102902, North Shore Mail Centre, Auckland 10

In India: Please write to Penguin Books India Pvt Ltd,
11 Panscheel Shopping Centre, Panscheel Park, New Delhi 110 017

In the Netherlands: Please write to Penguin Books Netherlands bv,
Postbus 3507, NL–1001 AH Amsterdam

In Germany: Please write to Penguin Books Deutschland GmbH,
Metzlerstrasse 26, 60594 Frankfurt am Main

In Spain: Please write to Penguin Books S. A., Bravo Murillo 19,
1° B, 28015 Madrid

In Italy: Please write to Penguin Italia s.r.l.,
Via Felice Casati 20, I–20124 Milano

In France: Please write to Penguin France S. A.,
17 rue Lejeune, F–31000 Toulouse

In Japan: Please write to Penguin Books Japan, Ishikiribashi Building,
2–5–4, Suido, Bunkyo-ku, Tokyo 112

In South Africa: Please write to Longman Penguin Southern Africa (Pty) Ltd,
Private Bag X08, Bertsham 2013